Poet Duet: A Mother and Daughter

by

Florence Adams Clark (b.1926)

and

Carolyn Clark (b.1957)

© 2019 Florence Adams Clark and Carolyn Clark.
All rights reserved.
This material may not be reproduced in any form, published, reprinted, recorded, performed, broadcast,
rewritten or redistributed without the explicit permission of Florence Adams Clark and Carolyn Clark.
All such actions are strictly prohibited by law.

Cover painting "Perry City Road" by William Benson
wmbenson.com
Cover design by Shay Culligan

ISBN: 978-1-950462-49-0

Kelsay Books Inc.

kelsaybooks.com

502 S 1040 E, A119
American Fork, Utah 84003

*for the mothers, daughters,
sons and fathers,
sisters and brothers
who cheer us on*

*and
especially for
Luisella and James Simpson,
"Clark Poems" Readers par excellence*

The selection of these poems was based upon a process of looking for signs of resonance. Few of these poems were shared mutually until now, and yet they have, remarkably, much in common. It is a pleasure to present them here, through Aldrich Press.

Let it be known that very early on, Florence's grandmother, 'Boma' Ober (who once lived in Horseheads, NY), through reading, writing and reciting, kindled in her granddaughter a deep passion for poetry.

Our present thanks goes out to friends and family, and especially to Beth (Elizabeth Clark Goldsmith) for encouraging this project. We hope that the whole "shared-family alphabet"—from Adams—Armstrong—Breen—Clark—Cullen—Goldsmith—to Scarboro and more—will enjoy reading and sharing this interlude.

A note regarding Acknowledgments: while *most* poems in "Part One: *Journeys* Intertwined" have been previously published, *many* in "Part Two: Unwinding" by Florence are new, as are a few therein by her daughter, Carolyn.

Acknowledgments

Florence Adams Clark

A Patchwork Quilt—The Writers Association of the Ithaca Area 60th Anniversary Anthology (1995): "Dad Clark at Ninety," "From the Cornell Plantations," "Parents."

Caring (Florence A. Clark, Ithaca 2011): "Caregiver," "Sitting Outside during a Heatwave."

Journeys: A collection of poems by Florence Clark (The WordPro, Ithaca 2003, 2017): "Battle," "High Noon before the Castle," "On the Train to Lausanne," "On the Train to Lausanne," "Early Morning Prayer," "Near the Falls in Winter," "In Rome," "Return Flight," "At the Airport," "For My Sisters," "Movement," "For My Grandchildren," "Witchcraft," "Moment," "Now," "Near Buttermilk Falls," "At the Airport," "Return Flight."

Songs of the Seasons (Florence A. Clark, Ithaca 1961): "A Moment's Monument," "First Signs," "Leaf Smoke," "Scene from a Pasture Gate," "Spring," "Winter."

Can We Get There by Moonlight? (The Poetry Group of The Writers Association, Ithaca, NY 1986): "Reconciliation," "Persephone at the Restaurant."

Carolyn Clark

The Avocet Weekly: "Young Woman Jogger."

Choose Lethe: Remember to Forget: "Beta."

Journal of Modern Poetry: "Crescent Trail Poem," "First Frost."

Mnemosyne: the Long Traverse: "Baby in White: le Petit Bateau," "Hike Alone: a Late Return," "Cameo in Rome," "Troy," "Alpha," "Porch Sitting Poem: Invocation to Mnemosyne," "Of Kerchiefs Waving," "A Letter from Colorado Grandad."

New Found Land: "Sarah's Nova Scotia Sky," "Six Wallflower Poems," "Stopping to Breathe."

Contents

Part One: Journeys Intertwined

For Poetry	8
A Moment's Monument	9
Scene from a Pasture Gate	10
Leaf Smoke	11
Winter	12
Spring	13
A Wedding Blessing: Islands of Delight	14
Battle	15
Wind: the Sea's Commander	16
First Signs	17
Baby in White: le Petit Bateau	18
High Noon below the Castle	20
Untitled	21
On the Train to Lausanne	22
First frost	23
Early Morning Prayer	24
Hike Alone: a Late Return	25
Near the Falls in Winter	26
In Rome	27
Cameo in Rome	28
Troy	29
Return Flight	30
Home Again	31
At the Airport	32
Clear	33
For My Sisters	35
Sarah's Nova Scotia Sky	36
Movement	37
For My Grandchildren	38
Spring Rain	39
Slim young limbs	40
Don't let man's evil mind	41
Dandelion Wishes	42

Sunset	43
Witchcraft	44
Young Woman Jogger	45
Moment	46
Porch Sitting Poem: Invocation to Mnemosyne	47
Now	49
Of kerchiefs waving	50

Part Two: Unwinding

New Ways to Love	52
Near Buttermilk Falls—November	53
Caregiver	54
Six Wallflower Poems	55
Sitting outside after the Heat Wave	58
Stopping to breathe	59
Walking through the old town with my son	60
For a little girl who dreams horses	61
Watkins Glen	62
Scotch Plaid	63
Dad Clark at Ninety	64
A letter from Colorado Grandad	65
Reconciliation	66
All Hallow's Eve	67
Persephone at the Restaurant	68
Alpha	69
Beta	70
Dinner Guest	71
Sick	72
On the Amalfi Coast	73
In Palermo	74
Crescent Trail Poem	75
Message in a Bottle	77

Part One: Journeys Intertwined

For Poetry

Some days
I wear you like a sash
tied across by chest.
When I run, you loosen,
swing back and forth,
almost untie yourself,
escape. Other days
you're sunflowers,
multiple, bright.
Then I stumble, dazed,
see my reason rushing by,
almost crazed.
How many lives
I've found in you,
lost: my fingers
        ache.

1986—FAC

A Moment's Monument

Hold fast this moment,
Feel its smooth circumference
Cupped within your hand,
Its wholeness quite unplanned
By man-made art.

Its certitude, its truth
Came lightening-winged, unannounced,
Effulgent with the soul's release,
And like a scattering of stars,
Did swiftly cease.

So rare the peace it brought,
And honey budded thought
As dear as springtime's instant glory,
And like that season too,
Sudden, sweet, and transitory.

1961—FAC

Scene from a Pasture Gate

If I could keep this sweep of hills in sight,
And breathe this space of quiet country road,
If I could catch the tempo and the might
Of that slow moving cart, its swaying load
Of grain, a golden autumn rain
Upon the wrinkled visage of this field,
If I could claim this all as my domain
And then walk back into the city, healed;
And somehow take those crimson maples there,
That flame against the season's brilliant blue,
To be forever mine, though unaware
I needed them, inevitably true.
But now the breeze turns cool upon my arms,
As shadows spread their wings on distant farms.

1961—FAC

Leaf Smoke

The smoke drifts in the hollows of the hills,
The village men are burning leaves tonight,
October evening and a setting sun,
And autumn's consummation skyward spun.

1961—FAC

Winter

Winter has no sound—
Wordless, denying all
With quiet petalled fall
On frozen ground.

1961—FAC

Spring

Once over I will write your name,
And feel the brightness in my soul,
The brook, untamed,
And full of sunlight.

The day that came too soon,
The daisies plucked for whom,
      They matter not—
I caught a skylark
And someday, somewhere, he
      Will sing for me!

1961—FAC

A Wedding Blessing: Islands of Delight

for Emily & Mas, June 2019

That you may always know
islands of delight,
with tide washed beaches
shining in the night,
the seagull's arch
above the buckled wave
and all the summer sweets
you crave for happiness.
So peace may keep your sleep
and speak in syllables of rain
on ribbon leaves outside your window pane.

2019—FAC

Battle

Above, the sky, remote and pure.
Below, the earth, steadfast and sure.
Between the two, the surging sea,
Fighting both for mastery.

Blue swell of wave, foam flung high,
White flash of challenge to proud sky,
The surge, the crash, the sounding roar,
Of wind-swept wave on earth's stone door.

1948—FAC

Wind: the Sea's Commander

for Sean

The wind is screaming orders.
The silence and calm is broken.
The sea does obey!
Here come the waves!
Again the sea
slashes the rocks below me.

> *Gutta cavat lapidem.*
> (A water drop wears out stone)
> Ovid—Epistulae ex Ponto IV, 10, 5.

Elba peninsula, 1967—CC

First Signs

Chalk marks on the sidewalk,
Bird song in the air,
Screen doors banging happily,
Children everywhere!

Hot-bright sun at naptime,
The whisper of a breeze,
Ruffling nursery curtains,
The hush-hush sound of leaves.

1961—FAC

Baby in White: le Petit Bateau

for Sarah

The space between
the snowflakes
is reserved for you.

You are dressed in white:
a *petit bateau*
your grandmother has given you

when you were a mere shower,
a *raison d'être*
a reason for being,

movement slowing down
before the final moment
of darkness gone forever.

"That is you!"
I can almost hear myself
saying to you,

in, say,
six years, when we look
at albums together.

You, the baby in white,
on a fleecy blanket
in an oaken crib.

You, the baby born
when Venus was rising
in a sun-slit sky,

just last week,
when purple was the buds
on the trees

and crocus and daffodil
pushed through
our pine bark garden.

You on the boat,
the little boat,
in a brave, mechanical sea.
Our waves were mapped like this:
broad and strong,
dry desert shapes
that brought you closer to brightness.

Not even then could I imagine
your whiteness, nor the way
one week fleeting past,

this quiet snow,
with flakes bigger than baby's eyelashes
would give me back to you,

a white sleep
while pink roses open their fullest,
embraced in baby's breath.

1994—CC

High Noon below the Castle

The blue dragon
has curled to rest
on the warm stones;
the tourists have flown
to nest in darkened rooms.
The white hotels—
as pure as marble columns—
have closed their shuttered eyes
against the sun.
There is no one
on the beach:
only a single umbrella
flowers—
out of reach
on the shimmering sand.

1960—FAC

Untitled

I lie on the sand
letting the sun seep into my body.

Is that a horizon?
One can never be sure.
The heat mists over my mind

and the shades of sea
choose no definite pattern for me.

Mykonos, 1971—CC

On the Train to Lausanne

The trace of that jet in the sky
is like the beginning of this poem,
another departure.
My companion resents my silence,
the way I roll back on myself,
full: the shimmering lake
floats memories
she cannot share.

Too soon
the conductor announces our stop.
"Get ready," my friend says,
"We're almost there."
And so my poem,
like that little boat
moving slowly out from the quay,
slips away without me.
But the lake,
the beautiful lake,
is still there.

1978—FAC

First frost

for Pindie

First frost
on the barbeque cover:
a milky way galaxy
on whose edge we live.
It's almost dawn,
the motion detector
lights come on,
the puppy pees—
water calls water—
say the Japanese.
Morning dishes stacked,
I turn on the dishwasher,
get ready to vote—it's Election Day,
whom shall I choose?

I choose you:
two mounds of Venus,
invoking *Monte Testaccio* in Rome,
mountain high piles
of pottery shards—not *ostraka*
casted for exiles.

We two crones who wear purple,
sipping warmed wine
by a steamy Swiss lake
where dawn still wears neutral colors,
and our lives are opaque
as the three far-flown daughters
who live outside us now,
at the edge of this our first frost.

2010—CC

Early Morning Prayer

for my mother, Florence Ober Adams

I am not alone.
You are here
in your rose covered tea cup
that would crack in my microwave,
and I am young, thirteen,
walking a high wall between poplars.
You are back home making breakfast,
waiting to applaud
my every attempt to shine.
At last I say, "Thank you."
Before this summer day
gathers heat and care,
gratitude fills my heart:

Did I ever say Thank you?
for giving me freedom,
                time.

1978—FAC

Hike Alone: a Late Return

I curse my own rising: words
obliterate song,
and light angles through leaves
to catch me, as I run on
like a long run-on sentence,
disobeying gravity, ignoring
time.

I came to the woods to make
sacrifice. I take back
a parched tongue, this scroll
and a mouth woozy with song.

1975—CC

Near the Falls in Winter

for my husband, Gardner

White branches
sharpen this wood:
birch slakes best,
is most in touch
with need.

Moss bubbles from the rocks;
icicles spin down;
only the caw of winter
flocks the air;

Yet suddenly your words
spring new skies:
you are walking through Florence:
I am there.

1978—FAC

In Rome

for Carolyn

In the National Museum
the best rooms are closed.
I think of those who must accept
each day's limitation—
Venus dethroned,
the Discobolus bled—
all those who wake
to the pleasure in ruins,
memories raising the dead,
treasures from some chipped past,
like the day you posed
for a poor artist's pen,
while your older brother teased,
tried to shake your silence,
your ceremonious calm,
older than Rome,
than Livia's fresco—
blue wash of sky
with bright wings flying—
your radiant childhood,
              my song.

1979—FAC

Cameo in Rome

Cameo-breasted Catherine
believes in grace
and divine beings.
they scrape her
as she falls
among the columns,
flinging a stone,
longing
for other belonging.

1977—CC

Troy

Blood drenched city
slave to blue knives
you are too awful to comprehend.
Troy, your Helen never knew
Iroquois ways, whose mirrors were
rippling pools.
No mica mirage
ever hung them
wall-wise.

1977—CC

Return Flight

for my mother, Florence Ober Adams

Taking off for JFK—
the last lap of my long flight
home, I remembered our years
in Manhattan,
how you always
dressed me in light:
your optimism, a revolving door:
I spun into sparkling lobbies
filled with green plants, life.

Yesterday, in London,
I visited Liberty's,
your favorite store,
and climbed the stairs to <u>Remnants</u>:
I looked for those roses
and the blue peacocks
you adored.

Afterwards, I found the park
and touched the trees,
their elephant hide like memories—
their grief pinched faces.
It was then you spoke:
"My dearest child,
fret not your cares:
Love is a trap for us on Earth
but the only means of measuring
               the way out.

1982—FAC

Home Again

Sleeping in
JFK's
air-conditioned confidence
I say:
Sister America,
I'm home again!

I've come through gates
and run from runways,
carrying home my heritage,
a sackful of dreams.

So what happens?
This morning "Greensleeves"
comes over the radio—
irreverent grocery store music
from a wealth of high halls.

Immigration took away my oranges
but let me through,
and as I enter this new port
a six hour old sun
is rising
to this new time.

1978—CC

At the Airport

We fly away,
are carried rather
more than less by fear
before take off,
a frightening dependence
on air, instruments,
and the jet stream.
      Yes,
I am unequal to
any parting that
pulls my heart up
in a bucket.
I cannot speak
to the man who fastens his seat belt,
nor see the child below,
trudging across the snow,
leaving only his footprints
for tomorrow's children.

1983—FAC

Clear

From this far away
it looks clear and simple,
a patchwork quilt
of cultivation:
fields harrowed
fields lying fallow
fields touching fields,
small differences.

Reading the mountain's ridges
is like interpreting photographic maps'
peculiar contours,
no space between the lines.

How easy from here, this high,
to forget the fluid markets,
sandal slap on stone,
the curb man's music.

How easy it is,
above the sirens' reach,
above the wail in human speech,
how easy it is
to forget
firstborn, the flute,
the waters' music.

Time changes as we chase the sun.
Even mountains' shadows shrink
leaving us more time
to think: infinitely mythical
we become less real,
more horrific.

We think ahead
to where we will be

so that
if and when
suspended animation stops
we might be
tucking our would-be children in bed
somewhere far off and secure
from the hum drum life of a hot dry land,
so that
if and when
someone shows us photographs
of our dreams—
illusive light that shines under our fingers
and is borne away
like sand by wind—
our hands that hold
the morning news
might not shake
nor grasp the reality
this world has to offer.

We say we are just
moved to tears
reading the ruin, that is,
fresh stuff like this
morning's news: a nightmare
of destruction.
We have let gravity pull
bombs to fertile fields
and people, dismembered
unfamiliar faces, are blown away
like angels,
poor devils.
      From this far away it looks so clear.
      And I can count the mountains' backs…like camels.
flying north of Israel 1978—CC

For My Sisters

Sometimes I feel as though
I've traveled so far
that a day can no longer
compress me,
squeeze me dry,
erase. Then I can stand
above Time,
as though on a mountain,
and peacefully survey
the valley of years,
that green plotted life—
                all mine.

1985—FAC

Sarah's Nova Scotia Sky

for Sarah G.

She walked alone to the wharf
   to watch the setting sun
and stayed long after to seize
   the foaming figurations
   water pouring over rock
   and the dappled sea

      turned
    a perfect star

1973—CC

Movement

So much of my life
I've been sleeping through the moonlight:
all that passion going on about me—
how I've ignored the stars.

Now, at last,
I'm waking up to darkness,
a country without borders,
with no one to question, surmise,
or shake down my silence
and see the mist rise.

The moon tonight,

slipping across the snow,
dissolving,
the full moon bled:
layers of fear—glazed ice,
like the moon escaping,
like desire fed.

1980—FAC

For My Grandchildren

The rain begins slowly
like a new poem
buried in my heart,
like what you try to tell me,
in fits and starts,
as the small leaves talk together,
and the round drops part.

2003—FAC

Spring Rain

for Anthony

Listen to the patter
Of the spring rain
Making droplets fatter
On the window pane.

Ithaca, 1967—CC

Slim young limbs

Slim young limbs
Reach for the blue above,
Their only hope,
The hope they always love.

For they know after what is coming,
After what man will do,
Their slim, young branches
Will never line the blue.

1969—CC

Don't let man's evil mind

Don't let man's evil mind
Ever, ever, ever find
Its way into nature's heart,
For that is when we'd have to
                part.

1969—CC

Dandelion Wishes

Too often as I am busy wishing
the puffs of grey depart unseen
and I am blind.

Lugano, 1971—CC

Sunset

The shadows of time deepen
until my window is only a mirror
of the past.

1971—CC

Witchcraft

This morning, clearing out
a space for contemplation
is like
carving out a pumpkin:
knife in and out,
then all that gunk.
Here an eye,
there another,
and then
that toothy smile.
Yesterday was easy:
I walked home from work
and remembered Yeats:
"She thinks, part woman, three parts child,
that nobody looks, her feet
practice a tinker shuffle
picked up on a street."
Witchcraft…Oh how I was
lifted off the ground!

1994—FAC

Young Woman Jogger

I know also
total abandonment,
both sides:

the sudden freedom
that comes in a glimpse
of the world's spaces—

your own breath
on a cool morning
as you run beneath
an avenue of trees,

or that moment when

somewhere in between

the beginning
and
the going on

we stop,
        falter,

find.

1980—CC

Moment

Sometimes,
when the new furnace clicks on,
I hear an airplane
revving for the take-off:
the warmth, the heat,
the kind compassionate heat,
and my life,
my beautiful white life,
my writing life
lifts off,
lands.

1995—FAC

Porch Sitting Poem: Invocation to Mnemosyne

Traditionally, Mnemosyne (Memory, mother of the Muses) was often invoked at the beginning of a long recitation

The muse is ready
the mind is able
legend, tall tale, myth or fable?

*Mnemosyne is gone to sea,
White sails, black sails.*

Teacher, teacher tell no lies,
spend more time on Her
before She turns leeward,
while the winds tug,
demand!

Before apron strings ache,
begin
by porch sitting:
backyard green, tin of rain,
be an apple
for her.

The muse as a child,
face pressing on fogged pane;
as girl,
splicing her split ends,
as woman,
wondering
when will forgetfulness sail in…

So begin!
before, as a mortal
she'll sit on the portal
asking woven wisdom
of her daughter,

asking *her* to tell
porch stories,
spell out laughter
rid the apple of its worm,
make her glow in turning
each shallow forever.

2013—CC

Now

for Carolyn

Thinking about you
like a shower of gold leaves.
In the deep woods
the sun lights up your path
making it more and more
significant.

Today I remember
your old lines:
"Of handkerchiefs waving,
mine tied to my bag.
Our hands move silently
to some God we have known."

2000—FAC

Of kerchiefs waving

(leaving my parents, the island of Giglio)

Mine tied to my bag.
Both of yours flew
silently to some god we have known.

1975—CC

Part Two: Unwinding

New Ways to Love

My unicorn bag upon your door
always tells you that
I have arrived.
On your window sill
the Matterhorn keeps watch.
I like to remind you
that once we climbed
to the little mountain hut
where the real climbers sleep
the night before their ascents.

Your room's lovely quiet
offers us rest,
and the flowers Betsy sent
and Tom's balloons lift us to your 94th…

This morning
I found you nodding off
in the activities room.
You were holding hands
with a woman also asleep.
I was glad.
A bell for you
rang in my heart
tolling our long love…

2011—FAC

Near Buttermilk Falls—November

for Cran and Carolyn

White branches
sharpen this wood.
Birch slakes best,
is most in tune
with need.

Snow webs the rocks,
the dim light chills,
only the caw of winter
flocks the air.

Yet suddenly
your words
spring new skies:
we are walking
through green times;
we are there.

c.2000—FAC

Caregiver

Freedom
   is a new dress
      I could slip on.
Now it hangs
at the back of my closet.
Sometimes
   it makes me cry.
      Then I understand
         why it does not
   console me.

2014—FAC

Six Wallflower Poems

for Michelle Montalbano's art show (lithographs)
Marlboro Gallery, Largo, MD

1. First Impressions

The dress is
headless,
no body,
yet
feet still
floating
in memory
of dances
torn
from a page.

2. *Wallflower*

Wallflower
is a compound word.
There are so many:
Invisiline fence
marked fragile,
instinctively clinging
to a wall,
blooming
just this once,
quietly, timeless,
fragile and fragrant
as a midnight rose,
alone
despite all the rehearsals.

3. *Dance of the Vein Dress*

Where's my body?
My buddy? Somebody?
Without partner
I am memory
Translucent,
Tangential,
Irrelevant.

The dance is over,
Yet still I hang,
Singing like a music box
When someone opens
the closet:

"Don't tread on me.
You are walking all over me.
My folds drip
blind crevasses of blood
for you who let me
fall
when we dipped."

What happened?
Why am I here?
Tendrils on a hanger,
left hanging.
I'm not
Ripstop,
you know.

4. *Earth tones*

Rivulets, taffeta, *tango* (means "I touch"),
I want dance, earth tones of Latin:
Salsa, mambo, merengue,
But here I am, headless, cold shouldered,
cleft and left
like a spring flower mown down
by the careless plow
at meadow's edge.

5. *Roots after all (Resolution)*

My Heroine, it's okay
to be a wallflower!

You are not a compound word,
this is not a jail or a closet or a wall
you are up against!

You are experiential,
experimental,
luminous, transcendent!
You are the forget-me-not dress
ever mindful of your roots,
and there you stay
through all the different
shades of the seasons,
growing strong,
growing wall wise.

2002—CC

Sitting outside after the Heat Wave

All I need
are those butterflies
and this breeze.
The morning offers both—
and a poem!

The drone of a plane
fades away.

I love the silence:
the blue sky
waits for prayer.

2012—FAC

Stopping to breathe

Stopping to breathe,
you envelop me
in your breath.

I am your watermark,
thin as paper,
shear as onion skin,
two-faced yet legible
as *Janus*
guarding the bridge.

Poems spring from silence
and little noises
that stretch time:

afternoon bird song,
the purr of a light plane
imagined beyond
pleated white blinds
make me think—
it must be a blue sky.

My daughter completed for me
the art of butterfly kisses
that I now pass on

to you: when, like trees,
we disentangle to grow
our separate ways,

remember these silences
timbered in peace
and desire.

2002—CC

Walking through the old town with my son

for Crandall

Walking with him again,
I seem to float,
or slide off roof tops,
fly. The blue sky,
the red bricks, the Court House,
its spires, even
the small tiffany window,
still there. Today, he points everything out,
everywhere, he uncovers
good memories,
and when he walks ahead,
looks back, laughs,
I recover happiness.
It catches fire,
flares.

c.2004—FAC

For a little girl who dreams horses

for Carolyn

I wanted her to get her wish,
her bunny-hunched wish,
her grass-sprung blade.
The colt, nibbling her fingers,
now, in mind only:
his breezy mane rippling,
as now,
beneath her hand,
she feels that quivering—
the body of her dreams.

1970—FAC

Watkins Glen

for Don C.—a birthday poem

Green life clings
to clean, raw ledges.
Light shakes the ruffled edges
of the falls. Shadows rub
the leafy faces—purring:
satisfaction is a long word.

Water deepens shallow pools:
stone endures, allows all.
Only the loose shale
is swept away,
and tomorrow,
like these steps
climbing out of the Glen,
rises out of today,
and is tenable
     again.

c.2010—FAC

Scotch Plaid

for Don—the view from Thompson Hospital

From here our colors are once again
blue and green: the treetops so close,
and clouds almost at eye-level.

> *Something old*
> *something blue*
> *something borrowed*
> *something new.*

Life, its joys and sorrows,
is what we shall wear
to this your final wedding:
a mysterious rendez-vous
whose *time and place*
are still unknowns.

For now, please take along
this view:
this tree-green coverlet,
and sea-blue blanket,
to the Lake nearby,
to that Castle
you four—my parents, you and J.—
used to frequent.

Tennis courts, well-watered greens,
Tommy Dorsey, snow capped scenes,
these are a few of my favorite things.

Don's list includes this:
know *where* to put a comma
and *when* to pause.

2013—CC

Dad Clark at Ninety

Last year,
the day after the first snow,
we walked in the country.
Finally you spoke:
"Listen to the quiet,
the quiet out here."
You saw a red leaf under the ice
and turned suddenly tearful.
"Where do I get my meals?"
you asked. "Where am I?"

At Blossom Hill
they publish a prayer:
"In whatever state
I am content."
All the way back there
you held my hand,
and at the door you told me:
"My horse's name was Gwendolyn.
I used to run and jump and grab her mane;
that was the only way
I could catch her."
Your eyes were all flight,
and I saw your mare
shoot out of her shafts
into nowhere.

c.1990—FAC

A letter from Colorado Grandad

Got a letter from my Colorado Grandpa
the other day.

He said he's sorry not to have answered
my letter sooner.

Says he's busy writing memoirs,
trying to remember,

setting them up for print,
everything he's ever found and lost.

Me, I laughed, felt just as guilty—
I'm busy too, in college, making

my own fiction.

1977—CC

Reconciliation

They destroyed the house,
and now,
they rebuild it piece by piece,
he at the upstairs window,
hammering against time,
nails down only
the known moment
and grinds his teeth at the garden,
alone in his forest eyes.

She on her knees in the closet,
choking the chortling weeds,
buries the root
of her sorrow
and dreams of a green
tomorrow, asleep
in the winter seeds.

1967—FAC

All Hallow's Eve

This time of year
the park is grey and stark
the iron trees,
antenna-like,
receive.

Scuffing through leaves,
I kick off the load
of blanketing mind
and walk up the road
to where the lake

shakes my connections
to cloud, branch, stone,
where even today's wall
seems ragged enough
to climb.

c.1967—FAC

Persephone at the Restaurant

Winter
shadows our talk.
The snow keeps falling,
and I drift,
see sadness approaching,
turning the corner,
dragging a sack of depression—
poor old rag woman,
lost and strange.

Blinking at your brightness,
I close my eyes, wish,
try to blow out my madness,
my longing to dance,
to flatten myself against you
and fatten like a snowflake
on one brief chance.

Words are too much.
You look away, gaze,
come back to me, rest.
My daughter, Persephone,
trapped in your dark maze,
cold as that green vase
placed between us,
shaping its own emptiness.

1986—FAC

Alpha

Shoring up fragments
stolen from Psyche's able
I am able to survive—
ambrosia lipped, forever stillborn.

Real gods don't bleed,
so the Greeks believed,
ichor enshrines their veins.

My own arterial heroes hide
in swift mercurial dreams:
Hermes' two-way mirror moved,

wading from my mind,
shattering death's threshold,
repaying me in kind:

a dream wedged between two eyelids
might well reveal the trembling blade,
his message crossed this *limen*
and now I live in shade.

1986—CC

Beta

Brush away erasure's flesh,
clear the table, rejoice:
Real god came to grant us choice
from soul's recessive sorrow, breath!

No more cliché latchkey children
and forgotten gloom.
Bring to light all fruition:
evil is but absence,
abysmal fear.

Into a well-lit room we march,
mercifully entrenched in tunnel vision,
like a knotted serpent offering fruit
in Asclepeion prescription,
unmindful of our sprawling roots,
the thirsting of a baobab tree
and our Little Prince.
What's a Classic?
Circuitous demands
traveling both directions
in chameleon-like blindness.

As the figworm wrestles
in its sea of similarity
blending into that womb
where expectations meet reality:

*just because you cannot see it
doesn't mean it is not there.*

1999—CC

Dinner Guest

I chatted, talked
and tried too hard
to cover the map,
for you were so shy,
young.
I had to release you,
see your trap
sprung.

And so I hung
a picture of my life,
a field in which you played,
and finally ran to me
and said,
"The mail must be delayed.
My mother doesn't write."

After you left
I watered the plant you gave me,
and brushed my hair:
I saw you there in the mirror,
quivering bright,
and heard you crying
while I held you tight.

c.1990—FAC

Sick

For one fathomless hour I listened
to your vomit on the phone:
at first it slithered through the holes

and then by some peculiar capillary action
it tumbled through the perforations:

over long fields of electric force
it was reduced to static
yet still seemed to me more power
than either a particle
or wave
or both

and it abandoned all rules

except for mass,
and thank god
for gravity,
the wires gagged
and buckled down.

1976—CC

On the Amalfi Coast

A daughter
walks her father
along the dock.
He stops and sighs.
That steep cliff
is like
his deep breath,
the way he surveys the coast
and reaches the end of it,
while the horizon
rests.

I see his world
passing away in intervals,
with music, grace,
in multi-terraced vines,
in the floating base of mountains
and cloud tossed pines.

c.1983—FAC

In Palermo

for Ben Zucchero (Gardner's interpreter during World War II)

Now, at eighty-three,
some terrible tenderness
in his smile,
in how he remembers
"his boys."

The three of us walk slowly,
stalking his long life.
those years in the States:
at seventeen, in Harlem,
lifting player pianos,
trimming hats:
a versatile Sicilian
banking his dreams
until Black Friday.
(He mentions it casually,
with grace.)

He has saved all our cards—
all those places we've forgotten.
He is like a temple facing the sea,
destructible, yet free.

Saying goodbye, we would hold him.
Our affection almost blinds us:
we stumble over his love—
he has to walk us away.

c.1974—FAC

Crescent Trail Poem

Running down the Crescent Trail
much warmer than I'd thought,
just before Dalecarlia Tunnel
wind zipped off my cap,
my hand caught
a spinning pinnate
brazen yellow.
Images fused like bone
clapped together over and over,
the slap of vertebrae shrinking,
expanding—a runner's dreamscape.
Why do we run?
We are captured in a dream:
Today's trail riddled with leaves,
our fortunes unstrained
in a bottomless cup of tea.

On the way back I stop cold:
a new bench, its bright plaque

In memoriam Jane Sisco 2008
  Long may you run

boldly etched, tells me everything,
explains the unanswered calls.
The last time I saw you was at our gym,
you were bruised wholly green,
told not to run any more,
going in for a brain scan.
That was the last time we spoke
until now—this brazen new bench invoking
a shock of tears, silent, insistent:
rest and go on. Why do we run?

To keep balance in our lives, seek peace
in jagged constellations underfoot.

Jane, *I saw the most beautiful things on the trail today.*
Shall I tell you?
Two deer eating among the kudzu undetected,
and the runners I saw today,
even before your bench found me
this warm November afternoon,
seemed unusually friendly.

2008—CC

Message in a Bottle

for Mother: Florence Ober Adams

Flying in
to your funeral,
empty plains
then Colorado
heaped below me.

Dad is there,
and somewhere,
between the airport
and the front door,
he has lost the key:
we have to break in.

On your walls,
all those pictures—
a photo album—
I am lost in its leaves.

In front of your mirror
I lift my hand:
you touch my hair,
revive
        our long
                affair.

FAC—1975

About the Authors

Florence Adams Clark spent her early childhood in the Rocky Mountain mining town of Gilman, Colorado. She left Colorado to attend Wellesley College, graduating in 1949 and moving with her husband, Gardner, to Ithaca, New York, where she raised a family and taught high school English. Florence has been writing poetry for as long as she can remember.

Carolyn Clark was born in Ithaca, NY as the youngest of three children, lived periodically in Italy, Switzerland and France. She studied poetry with her mother's teacher—Archie Ammons—graduated Cornell '79 B.A., finished a M.A. in Classics at Brown, and eventually completed her doctorate in Classics at Johns Hopkins: Tibullus Illustrated: Lares, Genius and Sacred Landscapes (1998). Her poetry publications include *New Found Land* (Cayuga Lake Books, 2018) and a pair of chapbooks *Mnemosyne: the Long Traverse* (Finishing Line Press, 2013) and *Choose Lethe: Remember to Forget* (Finishing Line Press, 2018). She and her husband, Geoff, both returned to the Finger Lakes region, enjoy visiting with family and friends.